Making the most of *HARVEST*

Contents

INTRODUCTION

Springing into autumn

As far as the calendar is concerned, it's 1 January. For the Inland Revenue, it happens on 6 April. But for the local church it is in September that the New Year *really* begins, with a buzz of new programmes to challenge people's restored energy levels.

Harvest

Harvest is often the first celebration of the new season. It is a traditional fixture and, as such, can provoke the question 'Why do we do it?' Our harvest celebrations originate in the peasant agriculture of the ancient Near East. The culture gap between the Old Testament world and our own may be unbridgeable: age-old rituals with sheaves of wheat mean little in a mechanized society. But many churches are rediscovering some surprisingly relevant truths in the principles underlying the practices.

Harvest, perhaps more than any other celebration, gets back to basics. By focusing on God as Creator and Provider it addresses the fundamental questions of all religions: Who are we? How did we get here? Why are we here and where are we going? And because it challenges us to acknowledge our dependence on the One who created all life, harvest demands that we examine the ways in which we relate to one another. It can be an uncomfortable time for the comfortably-off.

Hallowe'en

Recent years have seen the emergence of a very different kind of autumn celebration. Fuelled by the Hollywood horror industry, Hallowe'en has become increasingly popular. Beneath its apparently harmless surface of mild spookiness, lurks a sinister reality of occult involvement and distorted spirituality. Most worrying is the fact that the festivities are targeted principally at children and young people. Many churches are meeting the challenge not merely by preaching against it, but by offering positive and enjoyable alternatives to it, too.

Remembrance Day

As autumn moves towards winter, poppies appear and Remembrance Day is marked in almost every community. As well as giving opportunities for recognizing the self-sacrifice of those who lost their lives in conflict, the season provides opportunities to support and comfort all who bear the pain of bereavement.

The seasonal cycle of seed-time and harvest, the contrast between light and darkness, the joy of life and the sadness of death – these are just a few of the very 'live' issues uncovered by the traditional events of autumn. For any church the opportunities they present are endless. We hope that this book will help you start to make the most of them.

A JEWISH HARVEST

Roots

Jesus was a Jew; so were his disciples; so were the first Christians. The early Church began as a radical Jewish movement. Our understanding of our faith can be deepened and enriched by exploring its roots in the Old Testament and in Jewish culture. In recent years a growing number of churches have been rediscovering the 'Jewishness' of Jesus: in the process they have found a new depth to their understanding of his life and teachings and a renewed appreciation of the festivals of the Church's year.

Pilgrim festivals

Easter and Pentecost are closely linked to the first two of the annual cycle of 'Pilgrim festivals'. Easter coincides with Passover (*Pesach*) when the key event of Jewish history is commemorated: God's miraculous act of deliverance of his people from slavery in Egypt.

Christians celebrate the birthday of the Church at Pentecost. But it is also the festival of *Shavuot* marking the giving of the Law at Mount Sinai, when God confirmed his covenant relationship with Israel.

The Festival of Tabernacles

The Festival of Tabernacles (*succot* – 'shelters') completes the cycle. It reminded the people of their wilderness journeyings and their hope of a permanent home in the land of promise. In common with *Pesach* and *Shavuot*, it was also a harvest festival. While the earlier celebrations were linked to the grain harvests, *Succot* marked the 'in-gathering' of the crops of citrus fruits, grapes and olives.

At all of these festivals a faithful Jew was expected to journey to Jerusalem to worship at the Temple. But it was *Succot* which spoke most deeply of a pilgrim people's dependence on God as Guide, Protector and Provider. Its keynotes are thanksgiving and rejoicing. Its mood is one of celebration.

Making a *succah*

Families build a *succah* (shelter) outside their home to remind themselves of their ancestors' improvised dwellings in the wilderness. With a simple frame construction, the *succah*'s walls are made of blankets and its roof covered with branches of palm, willow and myrtle. It is decorated with the fruits and flowers appropriate to the season.

Throughout the seven days of the festival, families gather under the shelter of the increasingly wobbly *succah* for meals and celebrations. In warm countries they will sleep there. Tradition demands that the roofing branches be laid loosely enough for the stars to be visible between them.

Back to basics

Succot must be the most 'child-friendly' of festivals: how many other religious activities involve building a den? Through shared activity and family fun, the Feast of Tabernacles teaches biblical lessons common to both Jews and Christians: despite all our human ingenuity, we remain totally dependent on God for the basics of life – food and shelter. And despite all that we plan for ourselves, we only truly understand who we are in the context of our Creator's over-arching plan, which encompasses both the vast sweep of history and the everyday details of ordinary life.

A Hebrew harvest

Building a full-sized *succah* in the church would give a distinctive focus to a harvest family service. With careful planning the poles, blankets, leafy branches and fruits could be prepared so that children in the congregation could help build the shelter during the service. The traditional harvest gifts could then be displayed in and around it.

With some additional research, the theme could be extended to cover the whole weekend. For resources and further information contact The Church's Ministry among the Jews, 30c Clarence Road, St Albans, Herts AL1 4JJ, tel: (0727) 833114.

Readings

❑ **Leviticus 23:39-43 and Deuteronomy 16:14-15.** These passages give a clear description of the 'what, how and why' of the festival.

❑ **Psalm 118.** With its themes of dependence and deliverance, this psalm is closely linked to *Succot*. Verse 27 describes the Temple procession in which leafy boughs were carried.

❑ **Ecclesiastes.** This often-neglected book insists on the impermanence and vulnerability of human existence. It was read aloud as part of the *Succot* rituals. Ecclesiastes 3:1-15 ('There is a time for everything, and a season for every activity under heaven') would be an appropriate selection.

Prayers

'Praised are you, Lord our God, ruler of the universe, for keeping us in life, for sustaining us and for helping us to reach this moment.'
Traditional Succot *prayer*

While the Temple priests prayed that God would send rain, the people responded with the Hoshanah *('Help us!') prayer:*
'We beseech you, O Lord, save now! We beseech you, O Lord, make us now to prosper!'

Prayer of thanksgiving:
Who would not worship you, O Lord God,
O King most high?
Surrounded in glory you revealed yourself to
us and offered us the crown of your holy law.
You guided our fathers in the desert;

you spread out a cloud above their heads
to shelter them from the burning sun by day
and you kindled a glowing flame
to light their way by night.
You protected the tents that they set up
as their homes in the desert;
and so you demonstrated again
your great love for your people.

Jesus and *Succot*

John 7 shows Jesus taking part in the Feast of Tabernacles, in secret at first, but later choosing to make it the occasion for some of his most challenging and profound statements about himself.

The final day of the festival, the 'Great Day', saw the culmination of the prayers for rain. It was on this day that Jesus chose to say: 'If anyone is thirsty, let him come to me and drink' (John 7:37).

A CELEBRATION OF LAMMASTIDE

'The first of the first fruits of your ground you shall bring into the house of the Lord your God' (Exodus 23:19).

In-between days

For newspapers, it's the 'silly season'. For most children it means the one school-free month of the year. For families it's holiday-time. For the church, August is that 'in-between' month when many people are away on holiday and most activities are put on hold until September brings the return of 'service as usual'.

Things were different for our ancestors. Unlike most of us, their lives were closely linked to the rhythm of the seasons. Far from offering them the chance of a vacation, August marked the beginning of harvest – a time of urgent activity for the whole community.

'Loaf mass'

For many centuries 1 August was kept as the festival of Lammas (or 'Loaf mass'), when Christians dedicated the first gatherings of grain to God. It was the start of long weeks of hard work which culminated in the joyful celebration of harvest-home.

With its focus on God the Provider, Lammastide is a clear echo of the Old Testament practice of 'first fruits', when the people of Israel acknowledged their dependence on the Creator who had led them out of slavery and into the land of promise.

Based on Deuteronomy 18, the following outline was originally planned for Lammas Day services in the Norfolk village of Lammas, led by the Rev Di Lammas of CPAS. But the outlines need not be bound to the day itself. While offering any church the chance to explore the relevant aspects of an almost-forgotten custom, they can easily be adapted for use in conventional harvest services in September or October.

All-age worship service

Visual aids:	*Wool – a fleece or a handful of washed, unspun wool. Failing these, a soft-toy lamb* *Bread – the fresher and crustier, the better* *Wine – home-made from local grapes or other fruit if possible* *Oil – a small amount of high-quality olive oil would be best*

Opening hymn: 'Great is thy faithfulness'

Introduction to Lammastide

Bible reading:

Deuteronomy 18:1-5 or Leviticus 23:9-14. *(While the Deuteronomy passage concentrates mainly on how the Levites were to live on gifts offered by the people, it is made very clear that the grain, wool, wine and oil were offerings originally 'made to the Lord'.)*

Did you notice the list of things that were to be given to God? They were called the first fruits – the first grain, the first pressing of wine and oil and the first wool from the sheep.

First things are usually the best. Nothing tastes quite as good as the first strawberry, the first tomato or the first apple from the garden – or even the first cake that you eat from the batch fresh and hot from the oven.

God asks for the first and best of our produce and he promises that the rest of the harvest will follow in due course.

There's something exciting in this: God doesn't ask for anything that he hasn't already given us.

First fruits 1: The lamb and the wool

Along with the offering of first fruits an animal was to be sacrificed, usually a lamb. Sacrifice was a way of reminding the people that they were sinners needing forgiveness.

For us, too, there has been a sacrifice. Jesus died to give us forgiveness from sin for all time. What is sin? It is anything we say or do or think which is untrue, unkind or unloving – anything which falls short of God's standard and cuts us off from him.

And speaking of sin brings us back to the lamb and its wool. The prophet Isaiah wrote: 'Though your sins are like scarlet, they shall be as white as snow, though they are red as crimson, they shall be like wool' (Isaiah 1:18).

Sin is described as being bright red, scarlet or crimson, rather like blood which gets everywhere and is very hard to clean. Recently I mopped up someone's knee, when she'd had a nasty fall. It seemed that the more I mopped up, the more blood there was. There was blood on her clothes and blood on mine. When we got the dressings on, the blood still seeped through. It got everywhere and was pretty horrid. Sin is like that. Once you tangle with it, it grows and spreads. Tell one lie and the next one just follows. But God says that we can be cleaned up to be pure and white as snow or as a washed wool fleece.

God offers us forgiveness like pure new wool. So let's tell him now how sorry we are for the way we treat the things that he gives us.

Confession and words of forgiveness

O God our Father, we confess that we have often used your gifts carelessly, and acted as though we were not grateful. Hear our prayer, and in your mercy,
forgive us and help us.

When we enjoy the fruits of the harvest, but forget they come from you, then, Father, in your mercy,
forgive us and help us.

When we want the first share and the best portion for ourselves, and forget that Jesus said that the first would be last, then, Father, in your mercy,
forgive us and help us.

When we are full and satisfied, but ignore the cry of the hungry and those in need, then, Father, in your mercy,
forgive us and help us.

When we store up things for ourselves alone and do not give you your rightful share of our money and possessions, then, Father, in your mercy,
forgive us and help us.

Grant us thankful hearts and a loving concern for all people, through Jesus Christ our Lord. Amen.

Song: 'God forgave my sin in Jesus' name'

First fruits 2: The grain and the bread

The next first fruit to think about is the grain from which we get flour to make bread. I've got some fresh home-made bread here. Long ago God's people were asked to offer grain to God. It was later used by the priests to make their own bread. But listen to what Jesus said:

'I am the bread of life. He who comes to me will never go hungry... I am the living bread that came down from heaven. If anyone eats of this bread, he will live for ever' (John 6:35,51).

That doesn't mean that we'll never feel hungry again. But it does mean that if we let Jesus into our lives, then we shall never know the hungry feeling of a life without hope or meaning. With Jesus life has a purpose. We'll be living as friends of God now – and for ever.

Jesus gave his people a sign to help them remember all that he had done for them by his death. You might have thought he would have made up some amazingly exciting ritual to make sure we never forgot what he had done for us. But he didn't. Instead, he asked his friends to do something very simple: to gather together and share an ordinary meal of bread and wine.

Bread is all about friendship and fellowship. Did you know that the word companion means 'one who eats bread with another'? Sharing bread is about being together, being friends and caring for each other.

As an act of friendship, let's share this loaf now. I'll start it off at the front of the church. Break off a tiny piece for yourself and pass it on to the next person, until it reaches the back of the church. This is for everybody, grown-ups and children alike. It's a picture of our togetherness, but more importantly of Jesus, the Bread of Life.

Now we'll have some prayers to thank God for bread and all the other good things that he gives us.

Prayers of thanksgiving

For the warm sweetness of the fertile rain, for the hot days of ripening sun, and for the promise of harvest, we thank you O God, *and praise your holy name.*

For bread to nourish our bodies and all other foods that satisfy our hunger and keep us healthy, we thank you O God, *and praise your holy name.*

For those who work so that we might eat, from the farmers who produce the grain and meat right through to the people who sell it to us and cook it for us, we thank you O God, *and praise your holy name.*

For one another and the friendship we share, for friends at school and at work and in our local community, we thank you O God, *and praise your holy name.*

For Jesus, the Bread of Life, who satisfies our deepest needs, giving us life that will last for ever, we thank you O God, *and praise your holy name.*

For reminding us that when you ask us to give you our first and our best, you have already given us *your* first and *your* best when you gave us Jesus, we thank you O God, *and praise your holy name.*

For all your goodness to us, we praise your holy name as we say the Gloria together:

Glory be to the Father, and to the Son, and to the Holy Spirit, as it was in the beginning, is now, and shall be for ever. Amen.

Hymn: 'I am the Bread of Life'

First fruits 3: The wine

God asks us to give him our new wine. Here's a bottle of home-made wine that I brought with me today. But Jesus is ahead of me. He says that we have to sort out our lives to be ready for the new wine he wants to give us.

It's powerful stuff. In fact, when the disciples were given the special ability to speak in foreign languages at the first Pentecost, people thought they were tipsy. But Peter told them, 'These men are not drunk.' It wasn't too much wine. It was God's Holy Spirit giving them power and strength to live their lives differently.

It's a powerful new energy bubbling up inside us that Jesus promised. It means that we can live as God wants us to without struggling. We ask the Holy Spirit to take charge and give us his energy. It makes a tremendous difference to every aspect of life.

For example, first fruits: giving God the first and best of everything can sound like an awful chore. But if we ask the Holy Spirit to help, he changes our attitudes so that we can actually get excited about giving things away!

Giving to God needn't be a nightmare – it can be a joy if we let the wine, the power of the Holy Spirit, change our hearts. Putting others first isn't terrible – it's fun when the Holy Spirit helps us.

Prayers for a new way of living

Let's pray about this new way of living. We pray that the Holy Spirit may direct our lives in every way:

We ask him to guide us in our speaking so that all we say is loving and true.

We ask him to guide us in our witnessing to give us courage to tell people about Jesus.

We ask him to guide us in our giving so that we discover the joy of giving God his share of all that we have.

We ask him to guide us in our serving so that we might use his gifts for the good of others.

We ask him to fill our lives with joy as he makes us more like Jesus, in whose name we pray. Amen.

Hymn: 'One shall tell another'

First fruits 4: The oil

God asked his people for oil from the first pressings of the olive harvest. The olive oil in this bottle is top quality, very expensive, and, if I spilt it, it would get everywhere.

In many places the Bible speaks about God giving his people the oil of joy or the oil of gladness. The joy that God gives is different from just a feeling of happiness. Like oil, it seeps deep down into every bit of our lives. It eases the pain when bad things are happening to us, for oil soothes, eases and reduces friction. The joy that God gives can sort out broken relationships and heal differences between people. It won't necessarily bring loud laughter and backslapping, but it is something strong and reassuring deep within us.

Song: 'Give me oil in my lamp'

Isn't it amazing, God asks us for the first and the best of wool, grain, wine and oil. But look at what he gives us as well: forgiveness to make us clean as wool; the bread of life that satisfies for ever and unites us with each other; the power of his Holy Spirit like strong new wine to help us live for him; and the oil of joy to enrich our lives in every way.

Prayers for those in need

Our offering to God

Hymn: 'O Lord of heaven and earth and sea'

Prayer of blessing

BANNERS FOR HARVEST

Where to start

Look up the Bible references to harvest throughout the Old Testament, the Gospels and the letters of Paul. These will give you ideas for words to use on your banner. Poems and prayers, pictures, calendars and posters can also provide ideas.

Applying your ideas

With harvest, the challenge is to get away from the obvious. There's nothing wrong with the traditional images of wheat-sheaf, bowls of fruit and piles of vegetables – but it can be exciting to try something different.

- ❑ Think about the other resources of the earth: stone, clay, minerals, precious metals and gems.
- ❑ Consider the harvest of energy from fossil fuels, solar and wind power.
- ❑ Don't forget the missionary aspect of harvest, of sharing the seed of the word of God.
- ❑ You may want to focus on 'green issues'. God, of course, was the original conservationist when he gave men and women responsibility to care for the land he had given them.

Designing the banner

Simplicity is the keyword. A simple design, well done, will always be more effective than any amount of clutter. Take care with the lettering as the words are there for a purpose. They must not be swamped by the design – make sure they are legible from a distance. Add detail but avoid fussiness. The design can be true to life (see 'God, giver of all') or simple (see 'Give praise to God').

Making up the banner

Choose colours to express thankfulness and rejoicing. Yellows, golds and greens are the traditional harvest colours, but use other warm, earthy colours as well. Textured fabrics, stripes and checks can be very useful for depicting fields, which come in all colours today: yellow (rape-seed), red (poppies), gold (wheat), blue (flax) and, of course, green and brown. Floral fabrics with large patterns are good for flowers.

Back the fabric with iron-on vilene, and cut out carefully. Then appliqué on to background fabric.

The designs illustrated on the next page are an aid to get you thinking. They can be adapted in many ways to suit your needs. The lettering is shown in single line only and leaves you free to choose your own style for your banner.

THANKS
BE TO
GOD

All things come from You and of Your own do we give You

Give Praise to GOD

Forgive us, Lord, THIS WASTE

Our God is Faithful

LORD, give us thankful hearts

GOD Giver of all

Psalm 67 v6

Thanks be to God

THANK YOU GOD

The earth is the Lord's

Psalm 24 v1

The Fruit of the Spirit is...

LOVE
JOY
PEACE
PATIENCE
KINDNESS
GOODNESS
FAITHFULNESS
SELF-CONTROL
GENTLENESS

Galations 5v22

The ideas on this page may be adapted or used as shown. Rachel McHugh

God's riches Our resources

A GREEN HARVEST

Planetary problems

Regardless of political persuasion, most people will readily agree that humanity's relationship with its home-base planet is a troubled one.

Our record of stewardship for our God-given heritage is not good. Our rivers, seas and atmosphere are polluted; our forests are despoiled and our sources of energy squandered. All will agree that we could have done better.

By recklessly exploiting every available natural resource, the men and women of the northern nations have shown their almost boundless capacity for selfish short-sightedness.

Cause for concern

In a secular age, the environmental crisis provides the most easily communicable explanation of the nature of sin. The way things are now is obviously not how they were meant to be. The fact that they are not is clearly the result of human greed and opportunism. The evidence is overwhelming: men and women are responsible, both individually and corporately.

Again and again the Bible makes clear that, for human beings, right relationship with the environment goes hand-in-hand with right relationship with God. To acknowledge our dependence on our Creator, is to acknowledge our responsibility to care for his creation.

Think it through

Harvest provides the perfect opportunity to explore 'green' issues. Harvest can demonstrate that the Church has vitally important things to say on one of the most relevant of contemporary issues. There is no need for it to be a quaint survival of a Victorian village custom.

Of course, a 'green' harvest needs careful handling. There's nothing more depressing than being on the receiving end of endless examples of why the planet is in peril. People are left feeling powerless: 'Yes, I agree the situation is terrible – but what can *I* do about it?' It's important to leave people feeling that it is possible for the average Christian to make a practical difference – individually, communally and globally.

A green service

The following service aims to share a Christian understanding of ecology. It also provides a positive counter to the 'New Age' understanding which confuses the Creator with the creation.

Litany for the environment

Voice 1:   As we think about the place in which we live, let us first join with the psalmist in thanking God for his wonderful creation.

Voice 2:   Then let us hear his word of judgement on all those who threaten to destroy it.

Voice 3:   And let us also rejoice in the hope God gives for its future.

Voice 1:   The earth is the Lord's and everything in it: the world and all who
live in it; for he has founded it upon the seas
and established it upon the waters. (Psalm 24:1-2)

Voice 2:   The trees of the Lord are well watered,
the cedars of Lebanon that he planted.
There the birds make their nests;
the stork has its home in the pine trees. (Psalm 104:16-17)

Voice 3:   Who may ascend the hill of the Lord?
Who may stand in his holy place?
He who has clean hands and a pure heart,
who does not... swear by what is false. (Psalm 24:3-4)

Judgement on those who destroy the environment

Voice 1:   Let us hear the warning words of Isaiah.

Voice 2:   Woe to those who call evil good and good evil,
who put darkness for light and light for darkness,
who put bitter for sweet and sweet for bitter.
Woe to those who are wise in their own eyes,
and clever in their own sight. (Isaiah 5:20-21)

Voice 3:   Raise a banner on a bare hilltop, shout to them;
beckon to them to enter the gates of the nobles. (Isaiah 13:2)

Voice 1:   The Lord enters into judgement against the elders and leaders of his people: 'It is you who have ruined my vineyard; the plunder from the poor is in your houses. What do you mean by crushing my people and grinding the faces of the poor?' declares the Lord, the Lord Almighty. (Isaiah 3:14-15)

Voice 2:   Woe to you who add house to house and join field to field till no space is left and you live alone in the land. The Lord Almighty has declared in my hearing: 'Surely the great houses will become desolate, the fine mansions left without occupants.' (Isaiah 5:8-9)

Voice 3:   Woe to those who make unjust laws, to those who issue oppressive decrees, to deprive the poor of their rights and withhold justice from the oppressed of my people, making widows their prey and robbing the fatherless. (Isaiah 10:1-2)

Voice 1:   Who is it you have insulted and blasphemed? Against whom have you raised your voice and lifted your eyes in pride?

All: Against the Holy One of Israel!

Voice 1:   By your messengers you have heaped insults on the Lord. And you have said, 'With my many chariots I have ascended the heights of the mountains, the utmost heights of Lebanon. I have cut down its tallest cedars, the choicest of its pines. I have reached its remotest heights, the finest of its forests.' (Isaiah 37:23-24)

Voice 2:   Thus says the Lord:

Voice 3:   'Because you rage against me and because your insolence has reached my ears, I will put my hook in your nose and my bit in you mouth, and I will make you return by the way you came.' (Isaiah 37:29)

Hope for creation

Voice 1:   But the words of Job give us hope for the future.

Voice 2:   At least there is hope for a tree: if it is cut down, it will sprout again, and its new shoots will not fail. Its roots may grow old in the ground and its stump die in the soil, yet at the scent of water it will bud and put forth shoots like a plant. (Job 14:7-9)

Voice 3:   Let the fields be jubilant, and everything in them. Then all the trees of the forest will sing for joy; they will sing before the Lord, for he comes, he comes to judge the earth. (Psalm 96:12-13)

Voice 1:   You will go out in joy and be led forth in peace;
the mountains and the hills will burst into song before you,
and all the trees of the field will clap their hands. (Isaiah 55:12)

Voice 2:   We thank you, Lord, for the greenness of where we live.
We thank you, Lord.

All: The trees of the field shall clap their hands. Alleluia!
The trees of the field shall clap their hands. Alleluia!

(Adapted from the Kenyan Litany for the Environment, 1991)

LET EVERYTHING PRAISE!

All-age worship talk

Visual aids:
One large potato (with eyes)
One large ear of sweet corn/corn on the cob
One large bunch, or 'hand' of bananas
One large cabbage or lettuce (with a heart)
Large cardboard eyes, ears, hands (painted pink) and a heart (painted red)

Cut, bend and attach thick wire (perhaps a bent wire coat-hanger) with parcel tape to the back of the cardboard cut-outs. Bend and cut the wire so that about four centimetres sticks out, which can be pushed into the fruit or vegetable at the right time. You will need four volunteers to hold up the fruit and vegetables and their 'attachments'.

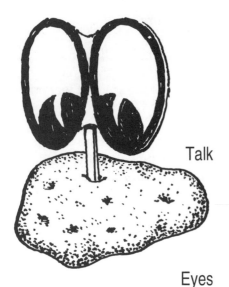

Talk

Admire the harvest display. Talk about the different fruit and vegetables, their colours, shapes and uses. Continue your talk by saying:

I thought we would let some of our harvest fruit and vegetables do the talking today. They remind us that God loves us, and how he wants us to thank him every day.

Eyes

A potato's eyes can't see. Ours can. (*Attach cardboard eyes to the potato.*) God has given us eyes to see all the beautiful world that he has created. But we get so used to many of his 'everyday' gifts of food, drink, clothing and shelter that we sometimes fail to notice them.

So, if suddenly there were no more potatoes, what would you miss most? (Answers may include chips and crisps of various flavours as well as roast, boiled, mashed, fried and baked potatoes.)

Let's thank God for eyes to notice all the good things he gives us: the rich shine on a juicy apple, the zingy yellow of lemons, the crisp green of lettuce, the soft pink of raspberries...

And let's ask him to help us look out for people who are hungry, lonely or sad. God relies on us to show his love to them.

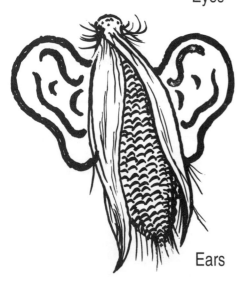

Ears

Corn has ears. But they can't hear much. (*Attach cardboard ears to the corn cob.*)

If everything made from corn and other cereals disappeared from your kitchen during the night, what complaints might you hear in your house tomorrow morning? (Encourage answers such as, 'Where's the bread / flour / cornflakes / pasta / cookies?')

Let's use our ears to listen out for reminders of God's goodness to us day to day – the sizzle of bacon frying, the crunch of toast, the pop of a cork from a bottle, the fizz of a refreshing drink...

And let's listen, too, for the sounds of people who need our help – some are shouting out in pain, others only whisper.

Hands

A bunch of bananas is sometimes called a hand. Somehow I don't think these fingers will ever learn to play the piano. *(Attach cardboard hands to the bunch.)*

Think of the fuzzy feel of kiwi fruit, the prickly armour of a pineapple, the stickiness of a toffee-apple.

We can praise God with our hands, by the things that we do. And while God loves to hear our prayers and praise, he cares most about what we actually do. Let's think of practical ways we can please him at home, at church, in the playground, in the classroom.

Heart

Who likes cabbage? Be careful of what you say – every cabbage has a heart. *(Open cabbage to reveal its heart and attach cardboard heart.)*

God cares very much about what we are like on the inside. Sometimes food can look great on the outside, but once you start to prepare it you realize that it's rotten in the middle.

God sees what we are like on the inside. He is able to change what we are like on the inside. *(See Romans 12:2: 'be transformed'.)*

Song: A good song to sing with this talk is: 'Praise him on the trumpet!'

CELEBRATING WITH UNDER FIVES

The tractor and the supermarket trolley

The book of Psalms gives us songs for all occasions: some of praise, some more personal prayers. The first eight verses of Psalm 65 contain some of the things that God has done for us. Look at them, and see how many you can list. Verses 9-13 show God's involvement in harvest. What are we told is the most important gift for an abundant harvest?

This activity is one of a number of CPAS Bible stories and activities for under fives from *Making the Festivals Fun*. The following songs might be appropriate to use with this story:

'My God is so big'
'Someone's brought a loaf of bread'
'Harvest is a time of food'
'Thank you Lord for this fine day' (make up a food verse)

The following visual aids will help you as you tell the story:

☆ a supermarket basket or shopping bag
☆ a very large shopping list with large writing and pictures, illustrating the food
☆ all the items on the list
☆ a tractor with a trailer, as big as you can find: if a child can sit on it, all the better, especially if you can dress the child as a farmer

Tell the story

Ask the children how many of them shop in the supermarket and ride in the trolley. Do they use a list to help them remember what they need? Show everyone your list: apples, bread, crisps, potatoes, carrots and milk. With the help of the children put the items on your list in your basket, e.g. show a picture of an apple, and ask someone to get one.

Remind the children that you start by singing. The Bible contains some songs, too, about harvest, when the people would thank God for his gifts of food to them throughout the year.

Story

Talk about the food you have collected, e.g. milk from cows, bread from grain, fruit from trees. Introduce a farmer and talk about how useful the tractor is. It pulls a trailer which carries bales of straw and food to the animals. It pulls the plough and the drill which scatters the seed. It also takes the grain to the big hoppers and the bales of hay to the barns.

The tractor and the farmer are important, but we still need God to send the rain and the sunshine to make the crops grow.

Make a tractor stained glass window

You will need
- ❏ red or green card: 1 A2 sheet makes 5 tractors
- ❏ black card
- ❏ greaseproof paper
- ❏ brightly coloured tissue paper circles, 10 cm diameter
- ❏ yellow or orange sticky or non-sticky paper
- ❏ water-based glue (not PVA) and brushes, or Pritt sticks
- ❏ pencils

Prepare in advance
- ❏ Cut out the template for the tractor, wheels and exhaust funnel
- ❏ Cut out the backing for the tractor in greaseproof paper, using the outer line of the tractor template.
- ❏ If you are unable to buy tissue paper circles, cut them out. You will need about fifteen per tractor.
- ❏ In black card cut out 1 large wheel, 1 small wheel and 1 funnel.
- ❏ In yellow/orange sticky paper cut out a large and a small inner wheel per tractor.

Get the room ready
Put out for each child/parent:
- ❏ 1 red or green tractor outline
- ❏ 1 greaseproof backing sheet
- ❏ 15 tissue paper circles
- ❏ 1 large black wheel and yellow inner wheel
- ❏ 1 funnel

Put out on the table:
- ❏ water-based glue and brushes (or Pritt sticks)
- ❏ pencils
- ❏ a few extra tissue paper circles

What each child/parent does
- ❏ Take the greaseproof paper tractor shape and glue on the tissue paper circles, making sure that they overlap.
- ❏ Take the red/green tractor outline and place it over the greaseproof paper. Once it is in position, glue it into place.
- ❏ Stick the yellow inner wheels on to the centre of the black wheels.
- ❏ Stick the wheels on to the tractor.
- ❏ Stick on the funnel.
- ❏ Cut away any coloured circles that hang over the edge of the outline. It is a good idea to do this while the children are playing elsewhere, or leave it to do at home. This saves having scissors around, and tissue is difficult to cut when wet.
- ❏ If you hold the tractor up to the light you get a stained glass effect. Suggest to parents that they stick the tractor to a window at home.

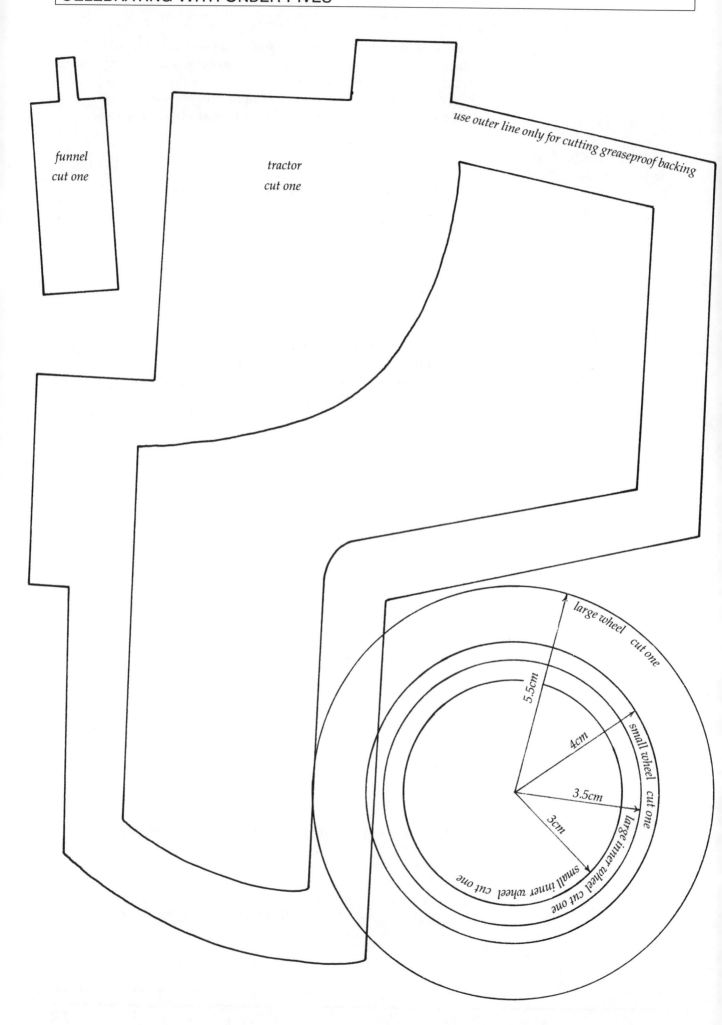

funnel
cut one

tractor
cut one

use outer line only for cutting greaseproof backing

large wheel   cut one

small wheel   cut one

5.5cm

4cm

3.5cm

3cm

large inner wheel cut one

small inner wheel cut one

HARVEST MISCELLANY

Country matters

In a town setting it takes hard work to make relevant links between the celebration of harvest and the daily experience of the community. In a rural environment it's much easier. When the year's work-routine is linked to the rhythm of the seasons it is not difficult to appreciate the 'working partnership' between God and humanity in the production of food.

This is how one rural church celebrated harvest:

'We are a valley community, fairly isolated. We felt that our harvest display should be special to us. We wanted it to reflect the produce of the area, as well as having the traditional baskets of fruit and piles of tins.

'We aimed to make a display that would have a big impact – with plenty of colour, diversity and quantity of produce. On one side of the aisle we had a trestle-table of the traditional harvest produce, but set out as a market stall – it made a better colour splash.

'Opposite this, on another table were items originating in our own valley where sheep farms predominate. The display included fish from a nearby trout farm, a large glass demijohn of water from the local reservoir and some timber from our Forestry Commission plantation. There were locally produced milk and eggs as well as a fleece. These were placed on bales of straw and blocks of local stone. A shepherd's crook was included in the display.

'It would be possible to incorporate this display more closely into the liturgy with a carefully prepared procession of gifts, with an appropriate prayer or reading for each item. The theme could also be developed in banners. Slides could be projected to illustrate some of the prayer topics.

'Being a small village, and having a large number of elderly people living on their own, we felt a good thing to do was to provide a lunch after the Sunday harvest service. More than anything else, we aimed to make our harvest festival relevant to the real life of a rural parish.'

We bring our gifts

How do you get the harvest gifts people have brought to church with them to the front? The following activity offers a solution.

Leader: As we bring our harvest gifts today we are obeying the commands for harvest time which God gave to his people in Old Testament times.

During the reading of selected verses of Deuteronomy 26, the presenter slowly carries an empty basket down the aisle and mimes the actions described.

Leader: When you have entered the land the Lord your God is giving you, take some of the produce of the soil and put them in a basket.

The presenter picks up each piece of fruit from the table in the centre aisle and holds each high for everyone to see before placing in the basket.

Then go to the place that the Lord your God will choose as a dwelling for his name.

The presenter lifts the basket high and walks to the front.

Place the basket before the Lord your God...

The presenter places the basket in the centre of the communion table.

... and bow down before him.

The presenter kneels in front of the table and stays there.

Leader: Now as we sing, you can come and bring your gifts to the front. Or you may have money to put in the basket during the song. When you have given your gift, you can kneel down with *(name of presenter)* here at the front, or in your pew.

Song: 'How precious, O Lord, is your unfailing love'

Gifts are presented and the offering taken during singing.

Leader: As the people of old, we say together:

All: *(Reading from overhead projector screen)* We have brought this sacred portion and given it to those who need it, as you have commanded us. So please look down from heaven, your holy dwelling place, and bless us. Amen.

Everyone returns to their seats.

Leader: As the people were reminded in the first Harvest Festival, so I remind you today: The Lord has declared this day that you are his people, his treasured possession as he promised, and that you are to keep all his commandments.

Symbols of harvest

These prayers may be linked to a procession. During the sung refrain a group of mixed ages, not necessarily family groups, bring forward symbols of the topic of each of the prayers.

As they bring forward their symbols, they stand facing the congregation on either side of the speakers. At the end of the prayers they place their symbols by the communion table.

The sung line could be spoken, if preferred.

Speaker 1: At this harvest time let us give thanks to God for his goodness and loving kindness to us.

Speaker 2: Let us also remember those in our community and in our world who are not so fortunate.

All sing: We thank you God for all we have, we pray for those in need.

Traditional harvest produce of fruit and vegetables is brought forward.

Speaker 1: Let us thank God for the products of harvest – for corn, wheat, potatoes, fruits and vegetables.

Speaker 2: Let us not forget those in countries ravaged by famine, drought or warfare.

All sing: We thank you God for all we have, we pray for those in need.

Garden flowers are brought forward.

Speaker 1: Let us thank God for the beauty of the natural world – flowers, trees, hills and mountains.

Speaker 2: Let us not forget the homeless people of our own cities, as well as those who survive in the shanty towns of the world's other great cities.

All sing: We thank you God for all we have, we pray for those in need.

Tins and packets of frozen or 'long-life' food are brought forward.

Speaker 1: Let us thank God for the technology which preserves our food so that we may enjoy it all year round.

Speaker 2: Let us not forget those who work in our local community helping those who at times have no food because they have no money.

All sing: We thank you God for all we have, we pray for those in need.

A lit battery-powered torch or lantern is brought forward.

Speaker 1: Let us thank God that our houses, schools and offices are warm and well lit.

Speaker 2:   Let us not forget those who have neither electricity, gas or firewood. Particularly we remember ordinary families caught up in civil war as winter approaches.

All sing: We thank you God for all we have, we pray for those in need.

A stand-pipe is brought forward.

Speaker 1:   Let us thank God that we always have clean running water from a tap.

Speaker 2:   Let us not forget those people from poorer countries who walk for miles for every drop of water needed in their homes.

All sing: We thank you God for all we have, we pray for those in need.

The offering plate is brought forward.

Speaker 1:   Let us thank God that we have money to buy the things we need.

Speaker 2:   Let us not forget those who have no money and are dependent for life on the giving of others.

All sing: We thank you God for all we have, we pray for those in need.

Speakers 1 and 2:   Father, Creator of the whole world, hear our prayers for Jesus' sake. Amen.

Good gifts

Narrator: At harvest we thank God for his gifts to us.

Son: Mum, you know it's Christmas soon?

Mum: Yes, dear.

Son: Well, Mum, you know Freddie next door?

Mum: Yes, dear.

Son: He's getting a motorbike, Mum!

Mum: *(As if she already knew)* Yes, dear.

Son: Well, Mum...

Mum: Yes, dear?

Son: Can I have one?

Mum: *(Without batting an eyelid)* No, dear.

Son: Ohhh... why not?

Mum: Because he's forty-three and you're only seven, dear. You wouldn't know how to use it.

Son: Oh. *(Thinks for a minute)* Mum?

Mum: Yes, dear.

Son: Can I have some Lego instead?

Mum: Of course, dear.

Son: Really? Wow!!

Narrator: In the same way your heavenly Father delights to give good gifts to those who ask him.

Bless this your world

Voice 1: Bless this your world:
The world you created,
The world you loved and died for.

Voice 2: Bless this our world:
The world that we live in,
The world that we share with each other.

Voice 1: Forgive us each day
As we live out our lives
With the parts that we hide from you.

Voice 2: And may we allow you to share in our lives:
The work, the joy, the rest, the fun,
The pain and the sadness too.

Harvest litany

Leader: For high street and superstore, checkout and cash-card
All: *We thank you, O Lord of our lives*

Leader: For commerce and industry, factory and workshop
All: *We thank you, O Lord of our lives*

Leader: For college and school, teacher and pupil
All: *We thank you, O Lord of our lives*

Leader: For policeman and fireman, doctor and nurse
All: *We thank you, O Lord of our lives*

Leader: For leisure and fun, recreation and sport
All: *We thank you, O Lord of our lives*

Leader:	For food and clothes, friendship and family
All:	*We thank you, O Lord of our lives*

Leader:	For spiritual food and the gift of your Son
All:	*We thank you, O Lord of our lives*

Leader:	For your kindness and love and a plan for our lives
All:	*We thank you, O Lord of our lives.*

Doing their best

This story is about the 'harvest of talents'. It involves audience participation. The words printed in bold capitals are cues for sound-effects – the louder and snappier, the better.

Use this list for a pre-story practice session:

COKE: *(Open can)* Fizzzz!
TRIP: Oops!
BEST: *(Punch the air)* Yeah!
ASSISTANTS: Yes, sir!
TRAMPOLINES: Boinnnngggg!
SWIMMING POOL: Splish splosh!

There once was a man who owned a leisure centre. It was the **BEST** leisure centre around, and it was run by the man's three **ASSISTANTS:** Dirk, Digby and Dougal.

One day the man decided to go on a **TRIP** around the world so he called in the three **ASSISTANTS** and said to them:

'I'm going on a **TRIP** around the world — and I want you to look after my leisure centre for me.'

First he put Dirk in charge of the **SWIMMING POOL**.

Then he put Digby in charge of the **TRAMPOLINES**, the table tennis and the **COKE** machines.

Dougal was put in the toilets, to look after them.

Then the owner told them to do their **BEST** and he waved goodbye and left.

It took Dirk ten seconds to decide what to do.

It took Digby ten minutes to decide what to do.

It took Dougal ten days to decide what to do – but he got there in the end!

Three weeks later the owner returned.

'Hello!' he said to his **ASSISTANTS**. 'I had a great **TRIP**. Now what have you been doing with my leisure centre?'

Dirk jumped up and said: 'I cleaned the **SWIMMING POOL** every day, put in a brand new inflatable shark, rescued three people in difficulties and made £500 profit.'

'Well done,' said the owner.

Dougal jumped forward and said: 'I cleaned the toilets every day. I put in some brand new fluorescent toilet paper and some delicious chocolate soap, and I charged everyone twenty pence a minute to go in. Here's the profit – £200!'

The owner was very pleased when he saw they had done their **BEST**. Then he turned to Digby.

Digby said: 'I locked up the **TRAMPOLINES** so the children couldn't get at them, then I sat on the table tennis table and drank all the **COKE**. It was very tasty.'

'What?' said the owner, 'You mean you wasted all that time and money? Was that the **BEST** you could do?'

'Well, I think you work people too hard,' said Digby, 'and I felt like having a rest, and anyway I wanted to look after the **SWIMMING POOL**, not the **TRAMPOLINES**.'

The owner was so angry that he gave Digby the sack and threw him outside. But he promoted his other two **ASSISTANTS** and he gave them both a pay rise because he knew he could trust them always to do their **BEST**.

Harvest hymn

These words may be sung to Gustav Holst's tune 'Thaxted', as in 'I vow to thee my country'.

My neighbour is a nation; his cry for bread is clear;
The hungry world of Asia still waits for us to hear;
The families of India hold out their hands for grain;
The cyclone's devastation brings Bengal pain again;
The anguished eye of parent looks down upon his child,
While carefully in London, my neighbour's need is filed.

The earthquake's grim destruction wracks Iran's heated land;
The fellahin of Egypt still plough their fields by hand;
The crowded camps in Sudan need more than special aid,
While men in Western countries try hard to be dismayed.
Yet standing with these people, the Christ I seem to see,
'Your neighbour is a nation; you did it unto me.'

O Christ of all the nations, I need your grace to share
Your bounty with my neighbour, my brother's pain to bear;
His burden help to shoulder, to stand where he must stand;
To spread the fruits of harvest – as you had always planned;
His needs to keep before me, his hunger day by day.
I am my brother's keeper, I cannot turn away.

INTRODUCTION TO HALLOWE'EN

Harmless fun?

It doesn't seem long since All Hallows Eve was a fairly unremarkable occasion. We made lanterns from turnip-heads or scooped-out pumpkins. We gathered on misty evenings to bob for apples and shiver at spooky tales. With its air of ancient folklore, Hallowe'en seemed a quaintly innocent part of the autumn scene – enjoyable enough, but quickly forgotten as the excitements of Bonfire Night claimed our attention and our pocket-money.

Sinister celebrations

Times have changed. From as early as mid-September shop windows display a garish collection of ghoulish merchandise. Most of it is directly inspired by Hollywood horror movies; nearly all of it is targeted at the junior market. For one night of the year children are offered the chance of a total identity switch as they are encouraged to transform themselves into vampires, werewolves, zombies and creatures from the black lagoon.

The growing popularity of 'trick or treat' door-to-door visiting now brings a wide variety of night-time callers – from harmless mini-witches and wizards accompanied by parents, to rather more threatening gangs of youths taking their first steps in the art of extortion. In many neighbourhoods elderly residents dread Hallowe'en. Whatever charm it may have once possessed has been replaced by insecurity and fear.

Something to hide?

And fear has been compounded by a recognition of Hallowe'en's darker side. Rooted in pre-Christian religion, it has a long history of association with occult activity. In recent years an increasing number of Christians have challenged the assumption that Hallowe'en is nothing more than harmless fun. Why, they ask, should we allow our children to take part in a festival which, at heart, is profoundly anti-Christian?

Cause for concern

Others, less alarmed by the spiritual dangers of Hallowe'en, feel equally antagonistic to it. They see little point in encouraging activities which are steeped in the gruesome lore and language of the 'video nasty'. Recent much-publicized court cases have drawn attention to the connections between juvenile crime and unrestricted video-watching. Many concerned non-Christians would agree that it is becoming harder to make a convincing case for promoting Hallowe'en – it could damage our children's health.

AN ALTERNATIVE HALLOWE'EN

Don't touch

On the whole we tend to be quick to identify what we don't like. But when it comes to saying what we're in favour of, we're slower off the mark. Pasting a 'hands off' label over Hallowe'en is easy enough. Providing an alternative activity that's positive, attractive and enjoyable demands hard work and imagination.

Fortunately recent years have seen many churches rising to the challenge. The end of October now brings a crop of all-age activities which are drawing in children and young people regardless of whether or not they have any church background. Most take light and colour as their theme.

Give 'em the old razzle-dazzle

Children may well have such a good time that they will want to return next year. Given good preparation and enthusiastic leadership, the word will start to get round that the local church is *the* place for fun on 31 October.

The ideas that follow are borrowed from numerous Light Parties, Bright Parties and Rainbow Rumpuses. They can be adapted to a variety of church situations.

When?

While Bonfire Parties are generally celebrated on the Saturday nearest to 5 November, most churches feel it's important to offer an alternative to Hallowe'en on the actual night of 31 October. Some offer Saturday parties and activities as well. Others have organized a complete 'Bright Weekend'. A London church cancelled both morning and evening Sunday services in favour of a programme of games and activities for all ages lasting from mid-morning until early evening; there was a picnic lunch and the festivities ended with worship and Communion.

Advertising

It's important to make clear why you are offering an alternative to Hallowe'en. There's no need to produce wordy leaflets outlining twenty theologically sound reasons for banning apple-bobbing; but it is good for people to be made aware of some of the dangers of flirting with the 'occult fringe'.

Here's a flyer produced by a large church in central London:

I've got A BRIGHT IDEA!

How would you like to enjoy a different kind of Hallowe'en party?

.... THE BRIGHT PARTY!!!

.....a dazzlingly brilliant alternative to the dark and shady goings-on normally associated with Hallowe'en!

But what exactly is a BRIGHT PARTY, you may ask ?

Hidden under the surface of Hallowe'en is the reality of occult power and satanic activity ...... we don't attempt to hide what the BRIGHT PARTY is all about: it helps children to enjoy "life in all its fullness" through fun and games, juggling and clowns, a bouncy castle .... happiness and laughter !!

So instead of a black cloak and hideous mask, why not dress up in fun, bright clothes and groove along to the BRIGHT PARTY!!

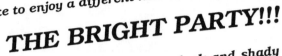 

Invitations

Many churches begin by planning Hallowe'en alternatives aimed at the age group they consider most vulnerable. But the pattern seems to be that before long they are arranging activities to include all ages. There's no reason why nurseries and Parent and Toddler groups shouldn't join in the fun.

Timing

Here's the Bright Party time-table adopted by one church:

a.m. / p.m.	3-4s activities linked to Parent and Toddler Groups
4.15 - 6.00 p.m.	5-7s party immediately after school
6.30 - 8.30 p.m.	8-11s Bright Party

The Youth Fellowship age-group organized their own party at a separate venue.

Decorations

You've decided to take light and colour as your theme? Then go for it! Forget about pastel shades. Choose day-glo colours and make your venue zing with fluorescent frenzy. Balloons and streamers are an inexpensive way of transforming any space with minimal effort. Encourage helpers to go over the top with their choice of clothes and – why not? – hair colour.

Programme

The three key ingredients for a successful party are entertainment, activity and food.

One youth leader said: 'We aim to have something happening all the time. While the children are arriving we have a clown or a juggler in action. We then get everyone together for a short welcome and maybe a quick drama sketch. After that we go into an all-together game or activity with the emphasis on co-operation rather than competition.'

All-together activities can include a variety of 'wide games'. One church features 'parachute games': racing, chasing, crawling and ball play under, over and around a second-hand silk parachute. The canopy can billow up or stretch taut according to how it is handled by the team holding it by the edge. (Further information from New Games UK, 28 Kendal Court, Shoot Up Hill, London NW2 3PD, tel: 081 452 2077).

Bouncy castles and other inflatables can be hired from Boing Creative Solutions, The Old Malthouse, 6 Pennywell Road, Bristol BS5 0TJ, tel: 0272 555544.

Many parties include a workshop session. The children split into groups and rotate around three or four fifteen-minute activities. Careful preparation is essential. Plan, prepare and rehearse so that you are certain the activity can be completed in the allotted time. There's nothing more frustrating than being hurried on to the next activity when you are only starting to get stuck in to the one in front of you.

Possible activities include: jewellery making, drama workshop, optical illusion 'spinner' toys, pop-up cards, symmetrical pictures with bright colours using the 'fold and press' method. One church organized an 'Egg Race Challenge' to see who could make the best elastic-band-powered moving model.

By the half-way point it's usually time for refreshments. Try to keep the colour theme going with your choice of ice-creams, drinks and snacks.

After the food it's probably wise to plan a relatively quiet activity. One leader said: 'At this point we do a short "talky bit": using a sketch or a story we aim to share why we are putting on this kind of party. We follow this with some lively all-join-in songs before ending with a disco session.'

HALLOWE'EN MISCELLANY

The following readings could be used in a pre-Hallowe'en service, or could be included as an 'extra' during an alternative activity.

The knock

I recognized the knock instantly. It was one of those tentative 'You go first!' knocks. One of those 'Go on, you can do it!' knocks. I'm sure 'Trick or Treaters' prefer doorbells.

I looked at the row of faces before me. Some wore painted masks of stolen lipstick and boot polish, some wore plastic creations from the joke shop. Others were just generally grubby, streaked from the autumn night games.

'Trick or treat!' The words rang out like a well-rehearsed anthem and twenty-four eyes glowed with mischievous anticipation. Of course they knew the response – I wouldn't dare refuse such a terrifying mob of Hallowe'en children. Sticky fingers and dirty boots would be the penalty should I fail the test. I shudder even now at the very thought. I smiled and made up my mind.

'Treat,' I said, and their greedy smiles lit up instantly. '*I'll* have a treat.' There was an uncertain pause. Eyes darted from side to side. I said it again, to reassure them: 'I'll have a treat, please.'

The spokesman of the group, appointed earlier behind the garden sheds, at last spoke up: 'Umm... a treat...'

I wasn't sure if this was a question or an answer.

'Umm...' Now he nudged the girl on his left who helped him out with a nervous giggle.

'Yes,' I said, 'I think I'd like a treat. In fact, I'm sure I'd like a treat.'

A dozen masks stared into their bin bag of goodies collected from other houses. Sadly a female arm dipped in to pull out a half-eaten bag of crisps.

By the time their faces peered up again at mine, I had returned with three mini Mars bars and a packet of peanuts.

It occurred to me as they scurried down the path that they loved the tradition of trick or treat, but weren't quite sure of its meaning. It was therefore quite easy to throw them into confusion by challenging their nervous beliefs and narrow expectations.

If only it were so easy to confound the real enemy at large...

Darkness and light

Speaker 1:	A reading for Hallowe'en
Speaker 2:	*(Leaping out from behind Speaker 1, wearing a Hallowe'en mask)* Boo! *(Speaker 1 jumps)* Scary, isn't it? *(Looks at mask)* Ugh! *(Throws it away)*
Speaker 1:	Shh! Stop messing about. Now – Hallowe'en...
Speaker 2:	*(Cutting in)* ... gives me the creeps!
Speaker 1:	Quiet! This is a serious reading.
Speaker 2:	Ugh – ghosties and ghoulies! Yuk!
Speaker 1:	Will you let me finish? This is important.
Speaker 2:	I can tell you all about that – it's about pumpkins and skellingtons!
Speaker 1:	Skellingtons?
Speaker 2:	Yeah, and trick or treacle and kids wearing bin liners!
Speaker 1:	No!
Speaker 2:	What?
Speaker 1:	No. It's not about all that.
Speaker 2:	Oh, yes it is. You ask the kids round our way!
Speaker 1:	No. Hallowe'en celebrates the dark side of the spiritual realm.
Speaker 2:	The damp side of the spittle and what?
Speaker 1:	Spiritual realm!
Speaker 2:	So you believe in all those ghosties and thingies then?
Speaker 1:	Yes. Some of it *is* real. But just because it exists, it doesn't mean that it is healthy and good. So we don't need to get preoccupied with it, do we? So please let me finish. Jesus said...
Speaker 2:	Hang on a mo! One minute you're talking about Hallowe'en, the next minute you're on about Jesus! Sort yourself out.
Speaker 1:	I am sorted out! There is a connection!
Speaker 2:	Oh yeah?
Speaker 1:	Of course. Jesus said that he was the light of the world and that whoever follows him will never fall into darkness.

Speaker 2:   So?

Speaker 1:   So that's the point. Hallowe'en celebrates the darkness. But Jesus is the light, the light of the world. His light shines in the darkness and the darkness has not overcome it. God is light – in him there is no darkness.

Speaker 2:   I'm confused – you've lost me. I thought we were talking about Hallowe'en.

Speaker 1:   No. *You* were talking about Hallowe'en. I was talking about darkness and light. In a way Hallowe'en is just a fancy word that represents things of darkness – fear, guilt and evil.

Speaker 2:   Ugh! Yuk!

Speaker 1:   Exactly!

ALL SAINTS' DAY

You don't need a halo to be a saint. The first day of November has long been marked as All Hallows Day. It is a time when the Church Militant (in other words all Christians now alive) celebrate their brothers and sisters in the Church Triumphant (in other words all Christians who have been 'promoted to glory'). Thanks to Christ's sacrifice for all of us, both groups share an extraordinary privilege: though all sinners, we are all equally entitled to call ourselves saints.

The following items look at the here-and-now pains and privileges of practical sainthood.

How can I live for you today?

I asked my Lord: 'How can I live for you today?'

He said: 'Dearly loved, take the shirt of my compassion, wear it close against your heart that you may love and lose, and hurting, heal and love again as I have done. And over all, wear love.'

I asked again: 'How can I serve you?'

And he replied: 'Wear kindness on your hands like gloves and do good, unseen things for others. Remember too my hands were pierced. And take gentleness as shoes that you may tread with quiet feet upon the hopes and dreams that weave like secret paths within another's life. And over all wear love.'

I asked my Lord: 'How can I be like you today?'

He touched and filled me and explained: 'Wear a tunic of humility woven on the warp that it is I who makes you holy, shot through with the weft of knowing you are proud. And tie a belt of patience round your waist that you may be held firm when others fail to see the princely robes in which I clothe you. And over this wear love.'

Once more I asked a question and smiling he replied: 'I am your coat of love. Gather me around you and take me too into your day.'

And over all was love.

Living saints

Peter
Paul
Mary
Martha
Matthew
Bartholomew
Silas
Mark

Augustine
Julian

Martin Luther
John Bunyan
John Newton
John Wesley
Lord Shaftesbury
Eric Liddell

David Watson
Mother Theresa

Jackie Pullinger
George Carey
David Wilkerson
Billy Graham
Brother Andrew
Terry Waite

We remember these for lives of love:
How will they remember us?

St Me and St You

Matthew taxed him.
Peter denied him.
Thomas doubted him.
Paul persecuted him.

James deserted him.
Mary wept for him.
Martha shouted at him.
Jesus never said a word.

He took their anger, frustration and failure,
Their guilt, their weakness and pain
And he made them all into saints.

I have all these 'qualities', Lord.
Can you do the same for me?

Love is...

Voice 1:   Love is patient and kind, it is not jealous or conceited or proud.

Voice 2:   It has survived the ages, and we have seen and testified to its rule in our lives.

Voice 3:   Love is eternal: from Adam in the garden to John in the new Jerusalem.

Voice 1:   Love is kind: like Noah inviting the people into the ark so they could begin again.

Voice 2:   It is strong: like Samson destroying the temple pillars, and Joshua breaking down the walls of Jericho.

Voice 3:   Love is fragile: like Moses in a basket, and Jesus in a stable.

Voice 1:   And it is gentle: like Ruth trusting Naomi, and Mary trusting Gabriel.

Voice 2:   Love is for everyone: five thousand on a hillside; twelve disciples by a lake; two travellers to Emmaus; one woman at a well.

Voice 3:   Love is broken: like Jonah in the whale, and Job on the scrapheap.

Voice 1:   It is honest: as David and his psalms, and Thomas and his doubts.

Voice 2:   And it hurts: like Jesus being whipped, and Peter weeping after cock-crow.

Voice 3:   Love is costly: like Abraham sacrificing Isaac; like Jesus dying on a cross.

Voice 1:   Love is alive! A curtain torn in two, a stone that's rolled away.

Voice 2:   Nothing can stop love.

Voice 3:   Love is eternal.

Voice 1:   And love is on your side.

ALL SOULS' DAY

A time to remember

Within the Roman Catholic church All Saints' Day is followed immediately on 2 November by the commemoration of All Souls' Day. It is an important day of prayer and remembrance focused on all the 'faithful departed'. Though naturally a solemn occasion, the mood is one of hopeful rejoicing.

In the Protestant tradition the day has had a lower profile. If all who have died in Christ are of necessity saints in glory with him, then surely there is no need for any commemoration other than that of All Hallows Day itself? But while there may be no strong tradition of special services and prayers for the dead, many are coming to recognize that All Souls' Day can be adapted to meet the needs of the living.

Living with loss

Late autumn seems to encourage quiet reflection. For many it can also be a time when the pain of bereavement is felt particularly keenly. When all the necessary activity of the weeks following a death have subsided, the long and lonely task of coping with loss really begins. A growing number of churches are finding that November is a particularly appropriate time to offer recognition and on-going support to those who have lost loved ones in the recent and not-so-recent past.

Recognition and support

Some churches now provide a special Memorial Service, to which all who have been bereaved in, say, the preceding twelve months are invited. The occasion need not be restricted to those who had a funeral service at the church, and, of course, those whose bereavement is long in the past may also welcome the opportunity to take part. But in all cases, the service will need thorough and sensitive preparation.

What follows is an adapted outline of one church's Memorial Service.

Memorial Service

Leader: We gather this evening to think and pray as we reflect upon those whom we love and who have now died. We have already commended them to God, but this evening we show our continued love as we remember with gratitude the gift of their lives to us.

As we do that, we pray for ourselves and our families, that we may know love and support and experience the truth of God's promise to be with us always.

Hymn: 'The King of love my shepherd is'

Opening Prayer: God of mercy, you are the hope of all those who put their trust in you. We praise you for all who have died in faith. We thank you for the assurance that you welcome them into your kingdom where there are no more tears and there is an end to suffering, and you raise them up in glory on the last day. We make our prayer through Jesus Christ, our Lord, Amen.

First reading: Romans 8:18-39

St Paul reminds us here that God has called us to share his glory and that nothing can separate us from his love.

Song: 'As the deer pants for the water'

Address

Song: 'Do not be afraid, for I have redeemed you'

Prayer: We remember, Lord, the slenderness of the thread which separates life from death, and the suddenness with which it can be broken. Help us also to remember that on both sides of that division we are surrounded by your love. Persuade our hearts that when our dear ones die neither we nor they are parted from you. In you may we find our peace and with you be united with them in the glorious body of Christ, who has burst the bonds of death and is alive for evermore, our Saviour and theirs for ever and ever. Amen.

A short time of quiet

The Commemoration

Leader: Glory and honour and power are yours by right, O Lord our God.

All: For you created all things, and by your will they have their being.

Leader: Glory and honour and power are yours by right, O Lamb who was slain.

All: For by your blood you have ransomed for God a kingdom of priests from every race and language, from every people and nation.

The leader now names all whose lives are being commemorated.

Leader: Jesus said: This is the will of him who sent me, that I should lose nothing of all that he has given me.

All: And I will raise them up at the last day.

Second reading: John 14:1-2, 6

Jesus speaks to his followers just before he is arrested, then crucified. He tells them to trust in God, even though everything seems so difficult.

Lighting of candles

Leader: We find it hard to let go of our loved ones and leave them in God's keeping. This lighted candle has been saved from Easter, when we remembered how Jesus rose from the dead to bring us God's new life. Tonight let it be a sign of the life and love of God. We invite you to come and take a candle and light it in memory of your loved one, and place it in the tray, so demonstrating your faith that all who trust in the risen Christ are in God's safe-keeping.

Music: 'Pie Jesu', from Fauré's *Requiem.*

When the last candle is lit, all stand.

Leader: Let us now say together in faith and trust the words that Jesus taught us.

All: Our Father...

Leader: Hear us, O merciful Father, as we remember in love those whom we have placed in your hands. Acknowledge, we pray, the sheep of your own fold, the lambs of your flock, and the sinners of your own redeeming.

All: We thank you that they are enfolded in the arms of your mercy, secure in the blessed rest of eternal peace and numbered among the glorious company of the saints in light. Amen.

Hymn: 'Thine be the glory'

Blessing and dismissal

Leader: The Lord bless you and watch over you; the Lord make his face shine upon you and be gracious to you; the Lord look kindly on you and give you peace; and the blessing of God almighty, the Father and the Son and the Holy Spirit be among you and remain with you always.

All: Amen.

REMEMBRANCE SUNDAY

The armistice agreement which ended the First World War was signed at 11.00 a.m. on 11 November 1918. In the years following it was at precisely that time each year that the whole nation stopped for two minutes of silent remembrance. After the end of the Second World War in 1945 the commemoration was moved to the Sunday following Armistice Day.

Sadly, since that time many more men and women have died in many more conflicts. While remembering the fallen, the living are challenged to re-evaluate their own commitment to peace. Despite the passing years, Remembrance Sunday still offers a poignant and important 'pause for thought' for the whole nation.

The Service of Remembrance, Reality and Reconciliation which follows offers a variety of approaches which may be adapted freely to individual needs.

Remembrance

Leader: We come together to worship almighty God, whose way is good. God's creative power sustains the world. His love enriches our lives, though we have often failed in our loving response. In Jesus Christ we can see the way to a new life, in union with God by the power of the Spirit in our hearts.

The way of Christ is a way of love, joy and peace. We who walk in this way offer up to God our whole being in service. We give thanks for the example of the saints and all who have lived out the way of Christ in the past.

We also offer to God all in whom this image of loving power and service has been disfigured by hatred, humiliation and war.

Old Testament reading: Isaiah 2:1-5; 10:33 – 11:9

Act of remembrance

Leader: Let us remember before God the men and women of all nations who have died as a result of war; those whom we have known and whose memory we treasure; those we never knew; and those who died unknown. We will remember all who have lived in hope but died in vain: the tortured, the innocent, the starving and the exiled, the imprisoned, the oppressed and the disappeared.

They shall not grow old as we that are left grow old: age shall not weary them nor the years condemn. At the going down of the sun and in the morning we will remember them.

All: We will remember them.

Two minutes' silence

Leader: Living God, by whose love we are united with one another across the boundaries of time and space, bring us to a new remembrance of your love and life, reflected in earth and sky, and every person who ever lived. Teach us to be reconciled to one another and to you, through Jesus Christ, our Lord. Amen.

Reality

Dramatic reading: Rich woman, poor woman

This is a dramatic reading for two voices. It is based on the turbulent experience of Chilean women during the revolutions of the 1970s.

I am a woman.
I am a woman.

I am a woman, born of a woman, whose man owned a factory.
I am a woman, born of a woman, whose man laboured in a factory.

I am a woman whose man wore silk suits, who constantly watched his weight.
I am a woman whose man wore tattered clothing, whose heart was constantly strangled by hunger.

I am a woman who watched two babies grow into beautiful children.
I am a woman who watched two babies die because there was no milk.

I am a woman who watched twins grow into popular college students with summers abroad.
I am a woman who watched three children grow, but with bellies stretched from no food. But then there was a man...

But then there was a man and he talked about the peasants getting richer by my family getting poorer.
... and he told me of the days that would be better, and he made the days better.

We had to eat rice!
We had rice.

We had to eat beans!
We had beans.

My children were no longer given visas for summer visits to Europe.
My children no longer cried themselves to sleep.

And I felt like a peasant.
And I felt like a woman.

A peasant with a dull, hard, unexciting life.
Like a woman with a life that sometimes allowed a song. And I saw a man...

And I saw a man. And together we began to plot with the hope of the return to freedom.
And I saw his heart begin to beat with the hope of freedom, at least...

Someday the return to freedom.
Someday freedom.

And then, one day...
But then, one day...

There were planes overhead, and guns firing in the distance.
There were planes overhead, and guns firing close by.

I gathered my children and went home.
I gathered my children and ran.

And the guns moved further and further away.
But the guns moved closer and closer.

And then they announced that freedom had been restored.
And then they came, young boys really...

They came into my home along with my man.
They came and found my man.

Those men whose money was almost gone.
They found all of the men whose lives were almost their own.

And we all had drinks to celebrate,
And they shot them all.

The most wonderful martinis.
They shot my man.

And then they asked us to dance.
And then they came for me.

Me!
For me, the woman.

And my sisters.
And for my sisters.

And then they took us
Then they took us,

To dinner at a small private club:
They stripped from us the dignity we had gained.

And they treated us to steak.
And then they raped us.

It was one course after another.
One after the other they came at us.

We nearly burst we were so full.
Lunging, plunging... sisters bleeding, sisters dying...

It was magnificent to be free again.
It was hardly a relief to have survived.

The beans have almost disappeared now
The beans have disappeared.

The rice. I've replaced it with chicken or beef.
The rice, I cannot find it.

And the parties continue, night after night, to make up for the time wasted.
And my silent tears are joined once more by the midnight cries of my children.

And I feel like a woman again.
They say I am a woman.

Act of penitence

Leader: Lord, you made the world and everything in it: you created the human race of one stock, and gave us the earth for our possession.

All: Break down the walls that separate us and unite us in a single body.

Leader: Lord, we have been divisive in our thinking, in our speech, in our action. We have classified, bombed and imprisoned one another; we have fenced each other out by hatred and prejudice.

All: Break down the walls that separate us and unite us in a single body.

Leader: Lord, you mean us to be one family, ruled by peace, feasting in freedom, freed from injustice, truly human, women and men, responsible and responsive in the life we lead, the love we share, the relationships we create.

All: Break down the walls that separate us and unite us in a single body.

Leader: Lord, we shall need ever new insights into the truth, awareness of your will for all humanity, courage to do what is right even when it is not allowed, persistence in undermining unjust structures until they crumble into dust, grace to exercise a ministry of reconciliation.

All: Break down the walls that separate us and unite us in a single body.

Leader: Lord, share out among us the tongues of your Spirit, as we repent of our misdoings, that we may each burn with compassion for all who hunger for freedom and humanness, that we may be doers of the Word and so speak with credibility about the wonderful things you have done.

All: Lord, forgive us; direct us in ways we do not yet discern and equip us for the service of reconciliation and liberation in your world, through Jesus Christ, our Lord. Amen.

Reconciliation

New Testament reading: John 15:9-17

Creed: We believe in Jesus Christ, crucified, risen and ascended, who has battled with evil and won. He has won with the power of his love, a love which is stronger than all the evil and violence in the world.

We believe in the power of his love, a power alive in his people today, a power to overcome fear and suspicion.

And we put our trust in his love alone, for we cannot rely on the weapons of this world when all our security, hope and life is in Jesus.

We believe in the power of the risen Christ, for only he can give us inward security. We turn away from all that is evil. We believe and trust in Jesus Christ our Lord and in the power of his love to overcome evil with good. Amen.

Prayer of intercession: We bring before God the needs of the world. We remember all who suffer as a result of war, poverty and oppression, all divided by barriers of race or nationality, of politics or religion.

Lord in your mercy, *hear our prayer.*

We pray for those parts of the world where there is tension and need of reconciliation. We pray for the work of the United Nations, its secretary-general and its agencies.

Lord in your mercy, *hear our prayer.*

We rejoice, O Lord, that you have made the earth so rich in natural resources. We pray that we may learn to use them responsibly. Not wasting them on what we do not need; not polluting the soil, the air and the sea; not wantonly destroying the life of animals and plants; but taking care to hand on to others an earth fit for the life of all to the honour of your name.

Lord in your mercy, *hear our prayer.*

We pray for all in special need at this time. Heavenly Father, your word teaches us that by bearing one another's burdens we may fulfil Christ's law. Help us to bring comfort, hope and love to those whose needs are so much greater than our own. Move the hearts of all who have it in their power to help to give gladly and freely. We ask it for the sake of him who gave himself to the uttermost, Jesus Christ our Lord. Amen.

Lord in your mercy, *hear our prayer.*

Act of penitence

Merciful God, we meet each other today at this cross, as inhabitants of one world.

As those who inflict wounds on each other,
Be merciful to us.

As those who deny justice to others,
Be merciful to us.

As those who seize wealth,
Be merciful to us.

As those who are greedy,
Be merciful to us.

From closed eyes that fail to see the needs of others, blind to opportunities of service and love,
Good Lord, deliver us.

From closed hearts which limit our affections to ourselves and to our own,
Good Lord, deliver us.

From the cowardice that dare not face new truth,
Good Lord, deliver us.

From the laziness that is contented with half-truth,
Good Lord, deliver us.

From the arrogance that thinks it knows all truth,
Good Lord, deliver us.

Lord, forgive our calculated efforts to serve you only when it is convenient for us to do so, only in those places where it is safe to do so, and only with those who make it easy to do so.

Father, forgive us, renew us, send us out as usable instruments that we might take seriously the meaning of your cross, for the sake of Jesus Christ, our Lord. Amen.

Stories and prayers of reconciliation: 1

In November 1992 at the village church in Huchenfeld in Germany a sobbing man fell into the arms of the deacon, saying, 'I was one of the Hitler Youth who killed them. Forgive me, but I do not have the strength to meet her.'

By 'her' he meant the tormented past suddenly brought back to life in this Swabian village. 'Her' was frail, seventy-four-year-old Margery Frost, the widow of Flight Officer John Frost who had been gunned down in the churchyard forty-seven years before. She was there to attend the unveiling of a tablet in memory of the five servicemen who had been killed. It had been raised by courageous local people. They had struggled to inspire their community to acknowledge their need to receive forgiveness for the past.

Margery said: 'All I have met with since I arrived has been warmth and understanding. People have taken me in their arms saying, "Please forgive us." I would like to have met the man who said he shot John. I wanted to give him my hand and say: "I have no bitterness anymore."'

The tablet reads: 'Father, forgive. Let the living be warned.'

Cruel actions have been carried out in the name of many religions and of many countries and for many ideals. Only by accepting our part of that inheritance can we help to purge it.

Prayer: O God of ages, the past so often haunts us, reflecting our weaknesses and displaying our folly. Grant us, patient God, the humility to look at all our yesterdays with honest and searching gaze, the courage to learn lessons and gather wisdom, and the commitment to face today and tomorrow with a zest to live loving and just lives, for the sake of your Son, our Saviour Jesus Christ. Amen.

Stories and prayers of reconciliation: 2

Simon Weston, a former Welsh Guard, served on the troopship *Sir Galahad* during the Falklands War. Fifty-one of his comrades were killed and he was extremely badly burnt when Carlos Cuachon, an Argentinean Air Force Lieutenant, dropped a 2,000 lb bomb on the ship. Simon has undergone forty operations and numerous skin grafts and has been left severely disfigured by his burns. In January 1992 he travelled with some of his colleagues to Buenos Aires to meet Carlos Cuachon. He said, 'I wanted to hate this man, but when it came to it, I couldn't.' It was an extraordinary moment, captured beautifully on television, when the two men met and embraced each other in an emotional encounter. Cuachon was so moved that he couldn't continue the interview. He said, 'I am so sorry for you and your family.' There was a profound reconciliation, beyond words and beyond understanding.

Prayer: O God, deal gently we pray with those who bear the wounds of this world's turmoil. In as much as we are perpetrators, name our evil and resist our wrongdoing. Be merciful and forgiving.

As victims, lavish upon us your healing and your love and such large-heartedness that we can escape the bitterness which kills, and soar free in the forgiveness which gives life, through Jesus Christ, our Lord. Amen.

■ Reference booklist

Further resources from CPAS

1994 CPAS Code	Title	Author and Publisher
03453	A Church for All Ages	Peter Greystone and Eileen Turner, Scripture Union
021698	The Dramatised Bible	Marshall Pickering / Bible Society
03524	A Voice in the City	Peter Hobson, Scripture Union / CPAS
03565	Bible Praying	Michael Perry, Fount
03418	For All the Family	Michael Botting, Kingsway
03483	More for All the Family	Michael Botting, Kingsway
03547	Drama for All the Family	Michael Botting, Kingsway
00391	Living with Loss	CPAS

Other books

	An Army with Banners	Priscilla Nunnerly, Ruth Wood, Nuprint / Christian Banners
	Unlocking the Future	Pedr Beckley, Lion

■ Acknowledgements

Many people have contributed to this book. Virtually all are active in local church leadership.

A Jewish Harvest: Church's Ministry to the Jews

A Celebration of Lammastide: the Rev Di Lammas

Banners for Harvest: Rachel McHugh

A Green Harvest: Trinity St Michael, Harrow

Let Everything Praise: The Church of the Martyrs, Leicester

Celebrating with Under Fives: Sue Kirby, *Making the Festivals Fun*, CPAS

Harvest Miscellany: 'Country Matters', St Andrew's Church, Slaidburn; 'We bring our gifts', St John's, Harborne; 'Symbols of Harvest', Holy Trinity, Ripon; 'Good gifts', 'Bless this your world', 'Harvest Litany', 'Doing their best', Dave Hopwood, *Time and Again*; Harvest Hymn, Paul Bunday

An Alternative Hallowe'en: St Paul's, Onslow Square, London

Hallowe'en Miscellany: Dave Hopwood, *Time and Again*

All Saints' Day: 'How can I live for you today?', Bridget Braybrooks; 'Living Saints', 'St Me and St You', 'Love is...', Dave Hopwood, *Time and Again*

All Soul's Day: St Margaret's, Thornbury; this service incorporates material from *The Promise of His Glory: Prayers for the Season from All Saints to Candlemas*, reproduced by permission of the Central Board of Finance of the Church of England; 'We remember, Lord, the slenderness of the thread...', Dick Williams, *Prayers for Today's Church*, CPAS

Remembrance Sunday: St Mathias, St Mark and Holy Trinity, Torquay; the 'Act of Penitence' and 'Rich woman, poor woman' are reproduced with permission from the World Council of Churches; Stories and prayers of reconciliation are quoted with permission from the Week of Prayer for World Peace.

Copyright © 1994 CPAS

Published by
CPAS
Athena Drive
Tachbrook Park
WARWICK
CV34 6NG

Telephone: (0926) 334242
Orderline: (0926) 335855

Church Pastoral Aid Society
Registered Charity No 1007820
A company limited by guarantee

First edition 1994
ISBN 1 8976 6021 9

All rights reserved. Permission is given for purchasers to copy the illustrations on to acetates for sermons and talks provided the CPAS copyright notice is retained on each sheet.

Compiled by Rory Keegan

Editorial and design by
AD Publishing Services Ltd
Illustrations by Doug Hewitt

Printed by CityPrint (Milton Keynes) Ltd

British Library Cataloguing-in-Publication Data: A catalogue record for this book is available from the British Library.